knock knock jokes

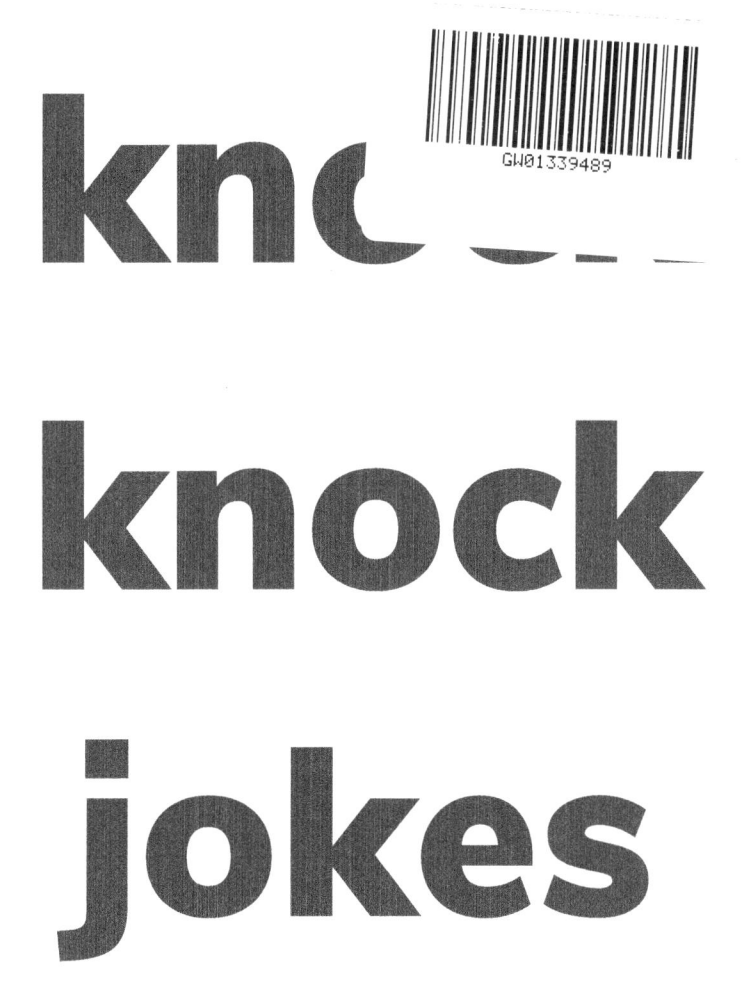

every
7-year-old
should know

Copyright © 2020 by Ben Radcliff

All rights reserved. No part of this publication may be reproduced, distributed, or transmitted in any form or by any means, including photocopying, recording, or other electronic or mechanical methods, without the prior written permission of the publisher, except in the case of brief quotations embodied in critical reviews and certain other noncommercial uses permitted by copyright law.

Introduction

Funny Knock Knock jokes have been around for a long time and making people laugh for ages. No matter what your age, kids, grandparents, adults and everyone in between can get a good chuckle out of a good joke. Granted, Knock Knock jokes might be a little corny and ridiculous but that's all part of the fun! These Knock Knock jokes have been collected with 7-year-olds in mind, but anyone can laugh at some of the best Knock Knock jokes of all time.

Read them straight through, skip around or play the Try Not To Laugh Game with these jokes. Can you keep a straight face and not laugh?

Try Not To Laugh Game Rules

Easy Version

1. Find an opponent or split up into two teams.
2. Team 1 reads a joke to Team 2 from anywhere in the book.
3. The person reading the joke looks right at the opposing person or team and can use silly voices and funny faces if they wish.
4. If Team 2:

 Smiles - (You see lip movement!) You get 1 point

 Grins - (You see teeth!) You get 2 points

 Laughs - (You hear noise!) You get 3 points

5. Read one joke at at time, then switch the giving and receiving teams.
6. The team with most points after five rounds wins! Use the score sheets on the following pages.

Challenge Version

1. Same rules apply except you get one point if you can make the other team laugh. No points for smiling or grinning.

Good luck and try not to laugh!

SCORE SHEET

	TEAM 1	TEAM 2
ROUND 1		
ROUND 2		
ROUND 3		
ROUND 4		
ROUND 5		
TOTAL		

	TEAM 1	TEAM 2
ROUND 1		
ROUND 2		
ROUND 3		
ROUND 4		
ROUND 5		
TOTAL		

	TEAM 1	TEAM 2
ROUND 1		
ROUND 2		
ROUND 3		
ROUND 4		
ROUND 5		
TOTAL		

	TEAM 1	TEAM 2
ROUND 1		
ROUND 2		
ROUND 3		
ROUND 4		
ROUND 5		
TOTAL		

	TEAM 1	TEAM 2
ROUND 1		
ROUND 2		
ROUND 3		
ROUND 4		
ROUND 5		
TOTAL		

	TEAM 1	TEAM 2
ROUND 1		
ROUND 2		
ROUND 3		
ROUND 4		
ROUND 5		
TOTAL		

	TEAM 1	TEAM 2
ROUND 1		
ROUND 2		
ROUND 3		
ROUND 4		
ROUND 5		
TOTAL		

	TEAM 1	TEAM 2
ROUND 1		
ROUND 2		
ROUND 3		
ROUND 4		
ROUND 5		
TOTAL		

SCORE SHEET

	TEAM 1	TEAM 2
ROUND 1		
ROUND 2		
ROUND 3		
ROUND 4		
ROUND 5		
TOTAL		

	TEAM 1	TEAM 2
ROUND 1		
ROUND 2		
ROUND 3		
ROUND 4		
ROUND 5		
TOTAL		

	TEAM 1	TEAM 2
ROUND 1		
ROUND 2		
ROUND 3		
ROUND 4		
ROUND 5		
TOTAL		

	TEAM 1	TEAM 2
ROUND 1		
ROUND 2		
ROUND 3		
ROUND 4		
ROUND 5		
TOTAL		

	TEAM 1	TEAM 2
ROUND 1		
ROUND 2		
ROUND 3		
ROUND 4		
ROUND 5		
TOTAL		

	TEAM 1	TEAM 2
ROUND 1		
ROUND 2		
ROUND 3		
ROUND 4		
ROUND 5		
TOTAL		

	TEAM 1	TEAM 2
ROUND 1		
ROUND 2		
ROUND 3		
ROUND 4		
ROUND 5		
TOTAL		

	TEAM 1	TEAM 2
ROUND 1		
ROUND 2		
ROUND 3		
ROUND 4		
ROUND 5		
TOTAL		

Knock Knock.

Who's there?

2:30!

2:30 who?

Tooth hurty,
take me to the dentist!

Knock Knock.
Who's there?
Cash.
Cash who?
I knew you were nuts!

Knock Knock.
Who's there?
Nana.
Nana who?
Nana nana boo boo.

Knock Knock.
Who's There?
Sarah.
Sarah who?
Sarah doctor in the house?

Knock Knock.
Who's there?
Olive.
Olive who?
Olive here, open the door!

Knock Knock.

Who's there?

Barbara.

Barbara who?

Barbara black sheep, have you any wool?

Knock Knock.
Who's there?
Howard.
Howard who?
Howard I know?

Knock Knock.
Who's there?
Aida.
Aida who?
Aida lot of sweets and now my stomach hurts!

Knock Knock.
Who's There?
Tekken.
Tekken who?
Why are you Tekken so long to answer the door?

Knock, Knock
Who's there?
Pudding.
Pudding who?
Pudding your shoes on before your pants is not a good idea!

Knock Knock.

Who's there?

Stopper.

Stopper who?

Stopper!
She's got my pickle!

Knock Knock.
Who's there?
Acid.
Acid who?
Acid calm down
and be quiet!

Knock Knock.
Who's there?
Atch.
Atch who?
God bless you.

Knock, Knock.
Who's there?
Rocky.
Rocky who?
Rocky bye baby
on the tree top.

Knock Knock.
Who's there?
Tinker Bell.
Tinker Bell who?
Tinker Bell is out of
order.

Knock Knock.

Who's there?

Russian.

Russian who?

Why are you Russian around the house?

Knock Knock.
Who's there?
Liz.
Liz who?
Liz roll,
we're going to be late!

Knock Knock.
Who's there?
Emma.
Emma who?
Emma cracking
you up, yet?

Knock Knock.
Who's there?
Buddha.
Buddha who?
I can't believe it's not Buddha!

Knock Knock.
Who's there?
A pile up.
A pile up who?
Ewwwwww...

Knock Knock.

Who's there?

Barry.

Barry who?

Barry the treasure where no one will find it.

Knock Knock.
Who's there?
Irma.
Irma who?
Irma big kid now!

Knock Knock.
Who's there?
Closure.
Closure who?
Closure mouth while you're eating!

Knock Knock.
Who's there?
Iran.
Iran who?
Iran over here to tell you this joke.

Knock Knock.
Who's there?
Pecan.
Pecan who?
Pecan somebody your own size!

Knock Knock.

Who's there?

Goat.

Goat who?

Goat to believe in magic.

Knock Knock.
Who's there?
Soar.
Soar who?
Soar you gonna open the door or not?

Knock Knock.
Who's there?
Noah.
Noah who?
Noah good place to eat around these parts?

Knock Knock.
Who's there?
Thermos.
Thermos who?
Thermos be a better Knock Knock joke than this!

Knock, Knock.
Who's there?
No.
No who?
No ifs, ands or buts, open the door!

Knock Knock.

Who's there?

Whale.

Whale who?

Whale, whale, whale what do we have here?

Knock Knock.
Who's there?
Stopwatch.
Stopwatch who?
Stopwatch you're doing and pay attention!

Knock, Knock.
Who's there?
Joe.
Joe who?
Joe King, I'm only Joe King!

Knock Knock.
Who's there?
Iron.
Iron who?
Iron these clothes,
they're so wrinkly!

Knock, knock.
Who's there?
Gladys.
Gladys, who?
Gladys the weekend,
no homework!

Knock Knock.

Who's there?

Pizza.

Pizza who?

Pete's a really great guy you know!

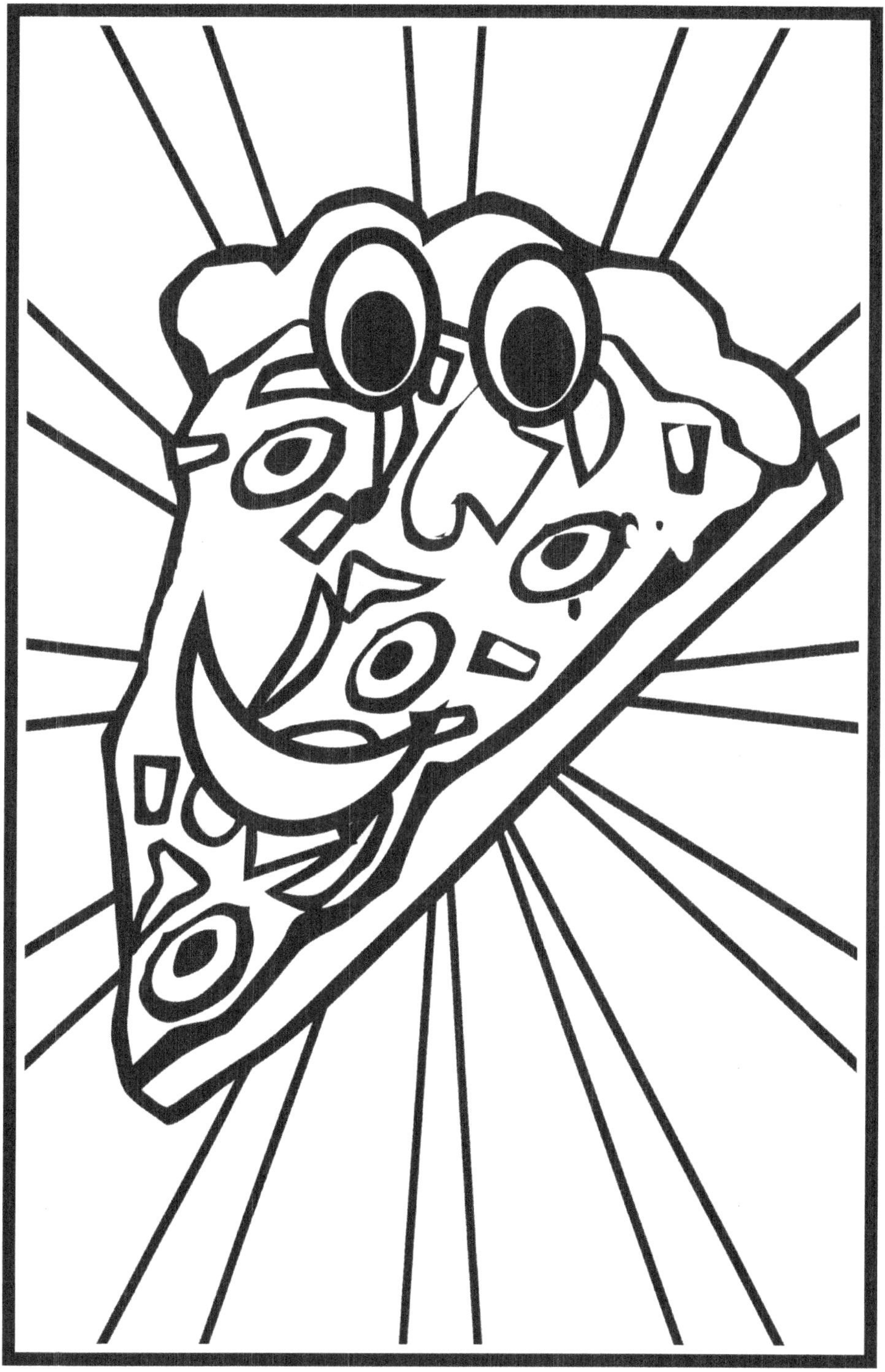

Knock Knock.
Who's There?
Juicy.
Juicy who?
Juicy how fast that cat was going?

Knock Knock.
Who's there?
Irish.
Irish who?
Irish you a happy St. Patrick's Day!

Knock Knock.
Who's there?
USB.
USB who?
U.S. bees make really good honey.

Knock Knock.
Who's there?
Rhoda.
Rhoda who?
Row, row, Rhoda boat....

Knock, knock.

Who's there?

Wa.

Wa, who?

Gee, aren't you happy!

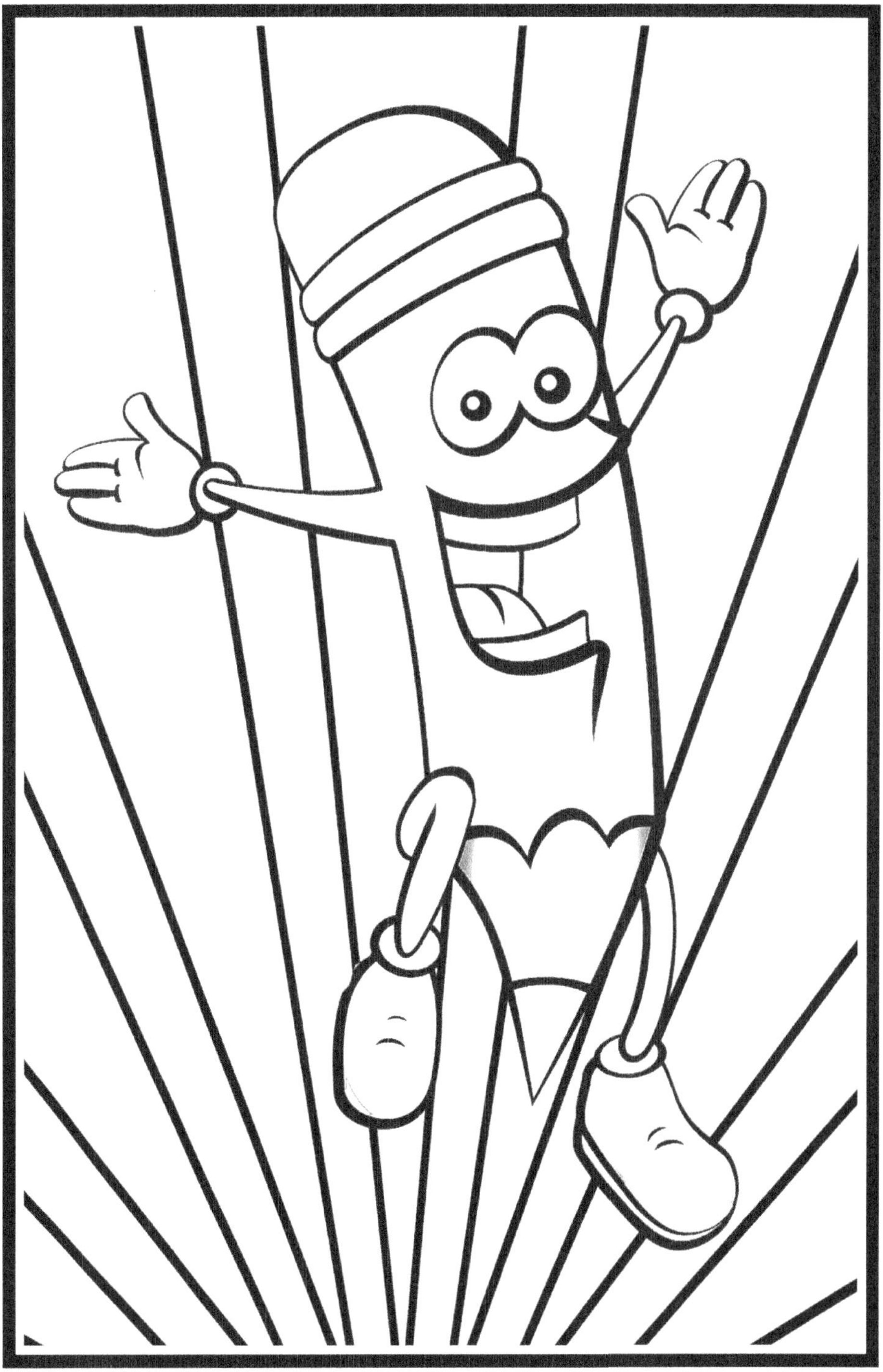

Knock, knock.
Who's there?
Annie.
Annie who?
Annie body home?

Knock Knock.
Who's there?
Tissue.
Tissue who?
All I want for
Christmas tissue.

Knock Knock.
Who's there?
Harry.
Harry who?
Harry up,
it's so hot out here!

Knock Knock.
Who's there?
Broken pencil.
Broken pencil who?
Oh, forget it
there's no point.

Knock Knock.

Who's there?

Rabbit.

Rabbit who?

Rabbit up carefully, it's a gift.

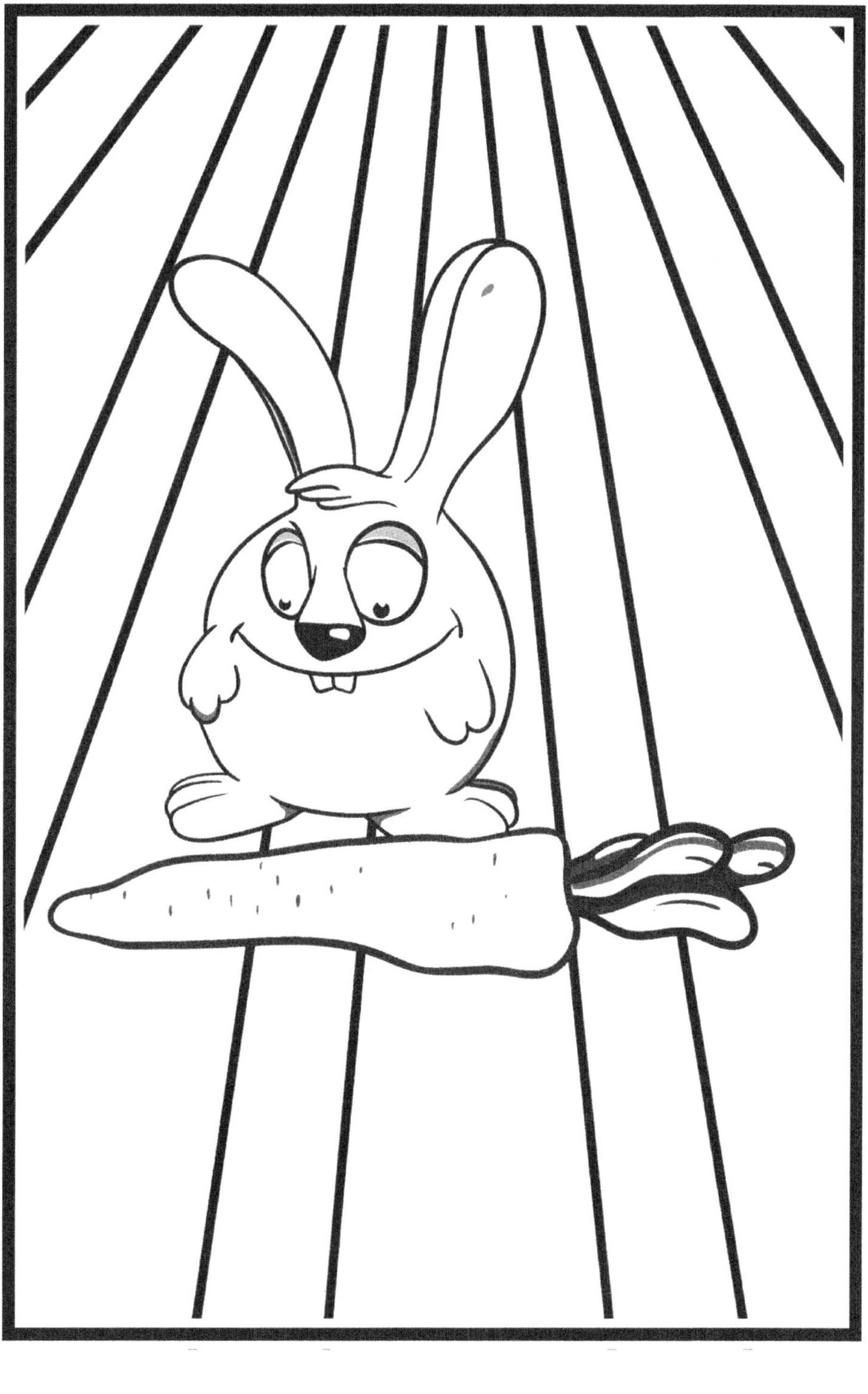

Knock Knock.
Who's there?
Stu.
Stu who?
Stu late to ask questions.

Knock Knock.
Who's there?
Dishes.
Dishes who?
Dishes a bad sign.

Knock Knock.
Who's there?
Wire.
Wire who?
Wire you asking, I just told you!

Knock Knock.
Who's there?
Willy.
Willy who?
Willy win or lose, that is the question!

Knock Knock.

Who's there?

Police.

Police who?

Police stop telling these awful Knock Knock jokes!

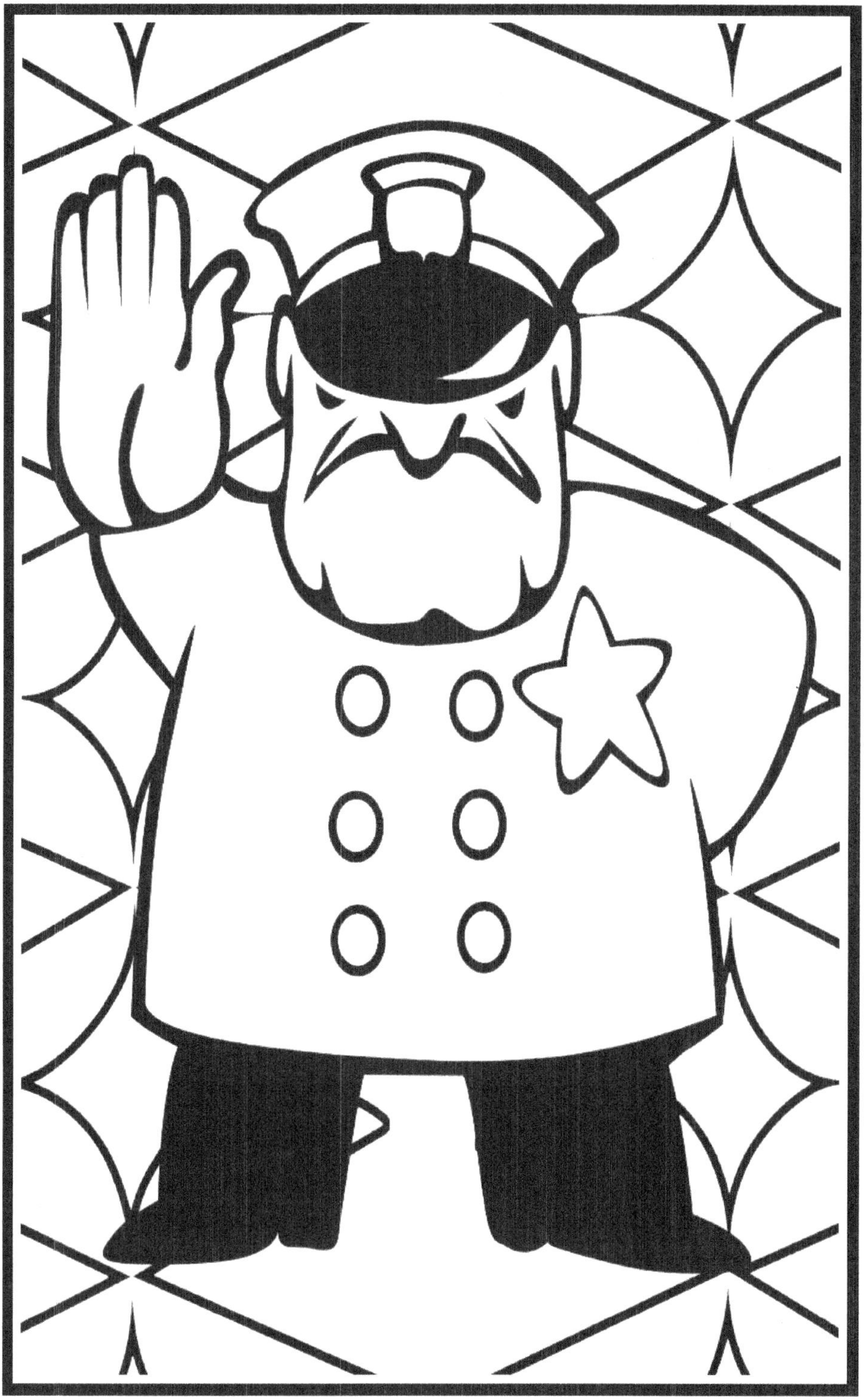

Knock Knock.
Who's there?
Ben.
Ben who?
Ben knocking so long my hand hurts.

Knock, knock.
Who's there?
Freeze.
Freeze who?
Freeze a jolly good fellow.

Knock Knock.
Who's there?
Mecca.
Mecca who?
Love Mecca the
world go round.

Knock Knock.
Who's there?
Dwayne.
Dwayne who?
Dwayne the bathtub,
I'm dwowning!

Knock Knock.

Who's there?

Thea.

Thea who?

Thea later, alligator.

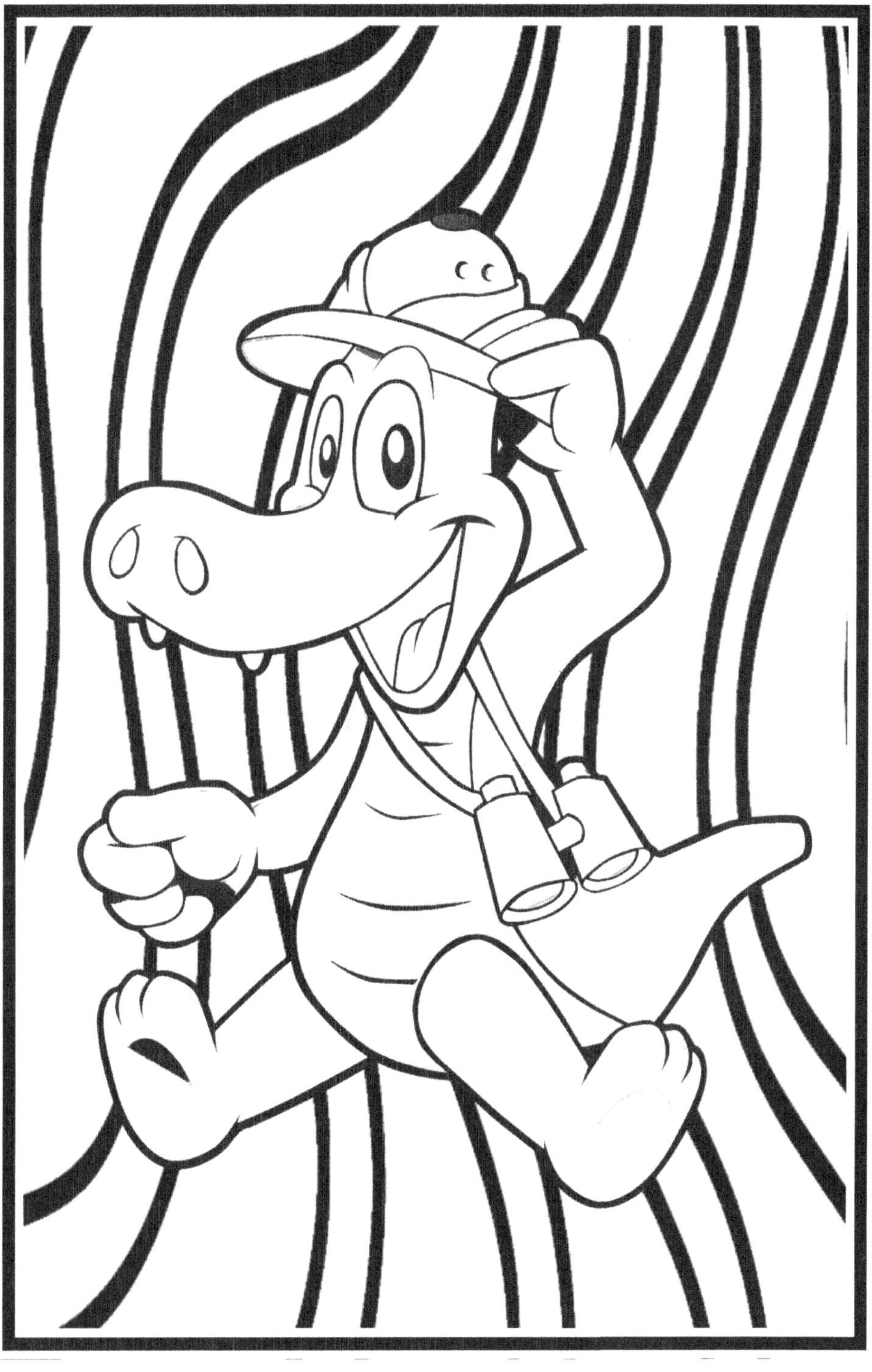

Knock, knock.
Who's there?
Artichokes.
Artichokes, who?
Artichokes when
he eats too fast.

Knock Knock.
Who's There?
Cozy.
Cozy who?
Cozy who is
at the back door.

Knock Knock.
Who's there?
Anna.
Anna who?
Anna one, anna two,
anna three...

Knock Knock.
Who's there?
Alex.
Alex who?
Alex the questions
around here!

Knock Knock.

Who's there?

Tuna.

Tuna who?

Tuna piano and it'll sound better.

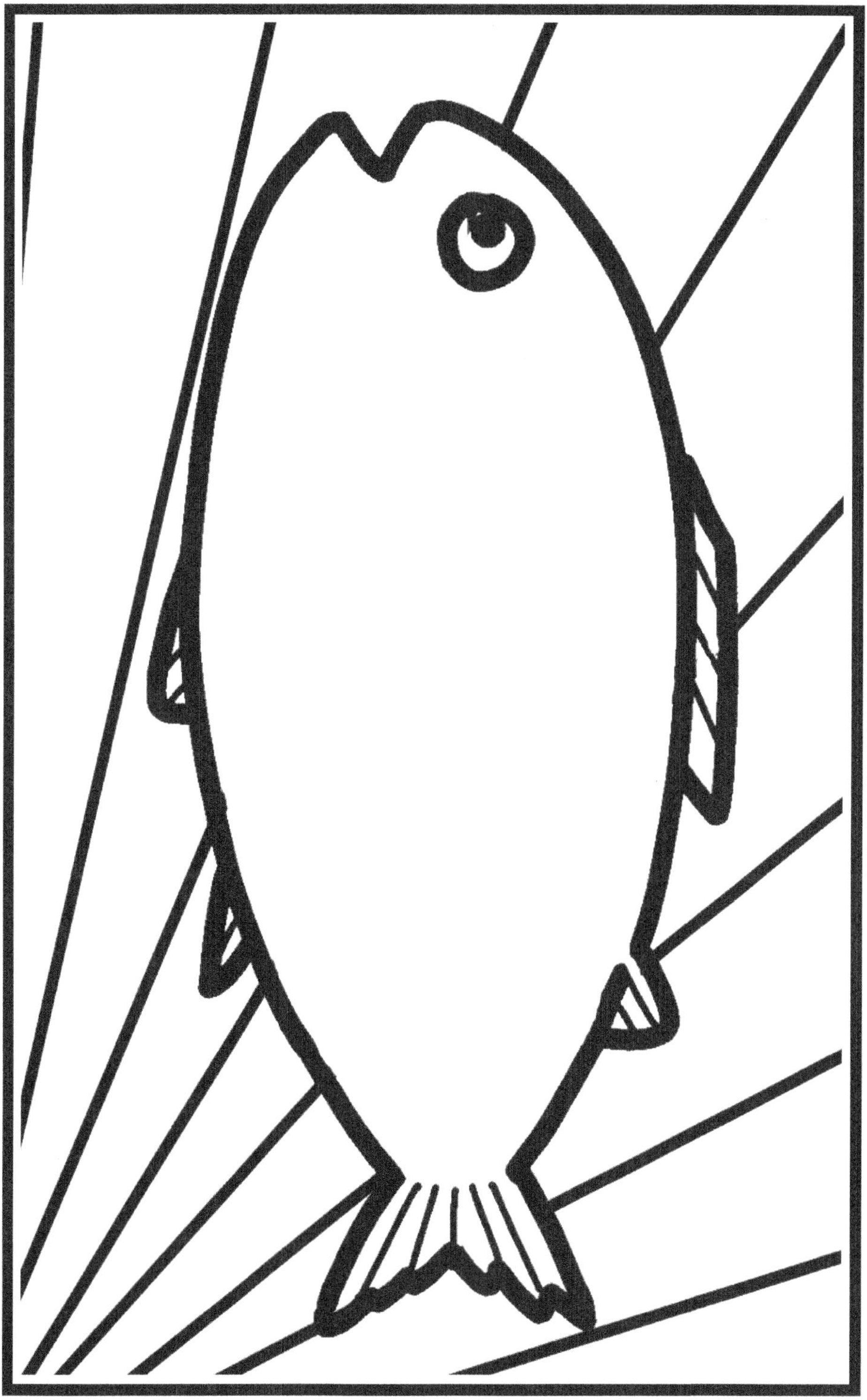

Knock Knock.
Who's there?
Mansion.
Mansion who?
Did I mansion you
have a nice house?

Knock Knock.
Who's there?
Oakham
Oakham who?
Oakham all ye faithful.

Knock Knock.
Who's there?
Rita.
Rita who?
Rita book for a change!

Knock Knock.
Who's there?
The door.
Oh wow, you can talk?